The View
from
My 80s

The View from My 80s

Poems by

Ruth Steinberg

ISBN: 9781080207442
First printing, 2019
Second printing 2019

Cover photo by Shutterstock
Cover and book design by the author.
Author photo by Barbara Hyde Haber

For my family
Barbara
Karen and Dana
John and Ying Lin

In loving memory of Ala and Audrey

Contents

x

Prologue

SISTER CHAIR

An old-fashioned lounge chair
sits among tufts of scrub grass,
put out to pasture
but not forgotten.
Its wrought-iron frame
rusted foot rest
speak of a finer past.
Its cushion – chintz, possibly,
with pink and green garlands –
is long gone.
Still, the armrests,
inlaid with delicately wrought ivy,
invoke an opulent yesterday.
The chair looks out onto the Sound
as months and years flow past.

I recognize my sister chair.
Although not so finely wrought,
my frame, too, has rusted in spots.
My cushion,
once green and plump
shrinks daily.
I, too, look out onto the Sound.

There
Comes
An Age

TELL ME

Is it like a lightning flash
a jagged ripping of a dark sky?
Or is it a slow accretion of hints
like a jigsaw puzzle coming together?

How is it to suddenly understand
how old you are?

TRANSITION

My friend Jean says I'm in transition,
that 80 is more than a milestone.
It's the start of a new phase of life.
Once I've accepted it, she says,
I will be at peace.

I have lived for more than 80 years;
that's old by any measure.
But while my conscious mind isn't accepting it
perhaps my subconscious is
for I've been simplifying my life
and it hasn't been difficult.

PARING DOWN

I will give away my mother's silver
and her convictions about everything.

I don't want my father's afternoon iced coffee
or his unfailing objectivity.

I'm throwing out my school report cards
and 50 years of calorie counts.

I will let go of my dream of a Pulitzer
or of winning the lottery.

I will give away my fear of heights.

But I will keep
my political rage,
all the books in my overflowing bookcases,
my banquet of loving friends.

And if I live long enough
I will publish undying poems.

THERE COMES AN AGE

There comes an age at which death
no longer requires much explanation,
writes the activist
Barbara Ehrenreich.

So and so died.
Oh? How old was she?
84.
Oh well, she had a full life.

How often I have dismissed
someone's death so casually.
And now, incredibly,
here I am at 84.

Were I to die tomorrow
my death
would require little explanation.
Oh well, I'm 84.

But I don't want my death,
when it comes,
to be dismissed with
oh well.

I require explanation.

Two old

Young Diana
when asked how old she was
held up two fingers and said
I'm two old.

Now it seems
I'm too old too.
Too old to give blood
said my doctor
who is not much younger.

I'm too old to fight commuter traffic,
too old to drive long distances,
too old to sleep through the night
without several trips to the bathroom.

Too old to cut the mustard
was a song in my youth
when I was not old enough
to understand "too old."

Now that I'm old enough
I still don't understand.

Carpe diem

A man died at 87 –
only three years older than I am now –
and I'm suddenly aware that
I probably have only a few years left.
For a moment
my impending death
feels frighteningly real.

I'm six short years away from 90,
an age I once insisted I didn't want to reach.
For a moment
the prospect of no longer being
is chilling.

Luckily such moments fade
as I go about my daily life.
I can't fix on what might be;
I'm too busy cooking my kale.

Who will I be?

Two years ago I leased a new car.
Will it be my last
before my lease on life expires?
How long will I still be driving?
Who will I be when I can no longer drive?

I've always been an authority
on spelling and grammar,
my "Webster" nickname fairly earned.
Now, increasingly, I am unsure.
Who am I if I can't spell?

Once I was Jeopardy smart;
now my answers
come slowly.
Who will I be when I have no answers?

As I age
my faculties age along with me,
some faster than others.

I am who I have always been

until I'm not.

AGE APPROPRIATE

It's only age-related memory loss
the neurologist said.
Quite normal for your age.

I think of my Uncle Wolf
whose memory loss
became full blown dementia
before he died at 95.
Was that normal for his age?

Does memory loss increase with increased
        age?
Do they go together
holding hands like Jack and Jill
as they fall and spill the contents of their
        bucket?
Or is there a point at which,
though the body keeps on aging,
the memory loss slows
or stops,
preserves what's left in the bucket?

BLANK SPACE

White noise
covers other sounds
provides privacy for intimate conversations.

White space
also called negative space
gives visual breathing room to thoughts on a
        page.

But the negative space in my brain when I try
to retrieve a memory

is not white

just blank

empty.

Like white noise
it covers up
what I am searching for.

Still, once white noise is turned off
other sounds are clear.

And when my blankness lifts, after I stop
        searching,
the elusive memory returns

after I no longer need it.

HOW LONG IS A LIFETIME?

Years ago I bought a lifetime supply of
dental floss;
it ran out but I'm still running.

When she was a young girl
my friend Jenny,
trying to be a helpful daughter,
ordered a dozen ironing board covers.
There's a lifetime awesome to contemplate.

When Jane turned 90
she gave away all her books
and waited to die.
Three years later
she's still waiting.

How long is a lifetime?
Too long for a family friend
who couldn't wait any longer
and drowned herself
in her bathtub at 100.

How long is my lifetime?
Will I go quickly
or linger?
Will there be pain?

When?

IDLE QUESTION

A symptom, a diagnosis,
an addition to my growing catalog
of pill-bearing ailments:
they no longer appear alone
but bring with them the question
(no fear, just curiosity)

Will this be the one?

Body Losses

Lost:
> two and a half inches in height –
> I am no longer tall by any measure;
>
> another molar –
> this one not worth replacing;
>
> confidence in dealing with technology --
> even downloading updates causes anxiety;
>
> the ability to sleep through the night –
> without a run to the bathroom.

But:
> I have also lost
> the excess pounds I carried for so long

so all that is lost is not a loss.

SIMPLE ARITHMETIC

The problem with having children
when you're young
is that they age
while you're still living.

I was 24 when John was born;
this year, when I turned 84,
he turned 60, Karen not far behind.

It's simple arithmetic,
but I find it
hard to understand.

DEATH AS PUNCTUATION

Someone once said
that at the end of every life
is a full stop,
and death could care less
if the piece is a fragment.

A life as manuscript,
death as punctuation.
How fanciful.
How   detached.
How   unemotional.

Most poets show no such cool detachment.
Keats called it easeful death;
said he was half in love with it.
Shakespeare's Hamlet wished for it devoutly.
That good night, Dylan Thomas called it,
although he did say wise men don't go into it
          gently.
Emily Dickinson had death
kindly stopping for her.
T.S. Eliot, always the exception,
waited for the death wind calmly,
likening it to a feather on his hand.

I don't expect my death
when it comes
to be poetic
and if it punctuates anything in my life
I don't expect to know it.
I do fervently hope, however,
that it is kindly and easeful,
and that I await it calmly.

I HAVE ALWAYS RUN AWAY FROM GRIEF

Afraid of such overpowering feeling
I would not let it touch me
except in brief bursts.

I didn't understand
that grief can be a quiet
companion to dailiness.

I found it easier to grieve
for literary heroines
than to feel my own losses.

Oh, I can describe them, but
even while writing this
my mind wanders to safer places.

But inevitably there will be
more and more losses;
the longer I live the more I will lose.

I don't want to be
a survivor.
I'd rather be someone else's loss.

NOTHING IS AS IT WAS

My cousin struggles
with advancing memory loss.
I leave her a voicemail message;
she's no longer sure she can retrieve it.
"But can I open it?" she asks me when we talk.

She, whose sharp-edged memories
sustained her lonely years,
now finds even
the past
is not
where she left it.

GENEALOGY

Before he died, Uncle Wolf could hear
nothing but baritone rumbles.
He lived to be 95.

In the end he was an infant again.
Memory gone,
all he did was eat and sleep.

His cousin Victor in Australia
at 100
is still himself.

My dad only made it to 70,
but he was all there
until the end.

And now I'm 84,
still myself,

but wondering ....

UNEASY LIES THE HEAD

It's the deeds
we wish we could do over,
to do them differently;
those are the deeds that come back –
not in sleep,
which could change their outcomes –
but in the moments,
or hours,
when sleep is slow to come.

Old regretted acts
make for wakeful nights.

PRESENT TENSE

When I pronounce the word future, the first syllable already belongs to the past.
                                    Wislawa Szymborska

Just saying the word, says Szymborska,
puts the future into the past

while Shakespeare tells us
what's past is prologue.

Future is past,
past is future.

This circular reasoning makes me tense.
Where, in their philosophies,
(as Hamlet would say)
is the present
that pop psychologists
tell us to live in?

Shakespeare and Szymborska are past;
pop psychologies come and go.

As for me
I plod along.
My past grows long.
My future is short
but still present.

FREEDOM

It's not retirement itself that brings freedom.
No, retirement often brings second careers,
new obligations.

It's aging
that loosens the strings that tie us.

We're on our own
to shape what time we have left
or not shape it at all
to feel free to say no
to read late into the night
to complete a poem
to know – or not to know --
for whom we write.

Habit

Just five minutes a day,
my nutritionist says
to get me back on the treadmill.
Then you'll establish a habit.

But habit isn't as reliable
as it used to be.
What once was automatic
now takes concentration.

Something has shifted
in my spatial orientation.
If I am not focused,
instead of taking a plate out of the cabinet
I will end up with a glass from the next cabinet.

If I intend to do two things
I am liable to forget one of them.

Still, I am doing my five minutes a day.
It's becoming a habit.

Just ten minutes a day,
my nutritionist says now.

Habit 2

A man I worked with
said you should always
find alternate routes to drive
so your brain doesn't become stale.
But he was young –
not yet old enough to retire.

The older I get
the more I find
habit keeps me functioning.
If it's not a habit
my stale brain may well forget it.

THE CONTENTMENT OF MY WINTER

Lady Diana Cooper,
who died at 93,
described her later years
as "a long unlovely wintry way."

But I find aging
neither wintry nor unlovely.
As for long,
the way grows short quickly enough.

These are in many ways
my best years,
earlier stresses
resolved or disappeared.

I have banished should
from my vocabulary.
I attend as I please
or decline as it suits me.

My time is mine to dispose of.
I permit myself to fritter it away,
to make space
for idle thoughts and musing.

My winter is a contented season.

MY UPSIDE-DOWN BUCKET LIST

Some people
when they get to be my age
think of all the things

they still want to do
before they die.
It's their bucket list.

I have a list too, not things I want to do
before I kick that bucket,
but things I no longer will do.

No more bra when I'm at home.
When I go out,
no pantyhose or high-heeled shoes.

No more big parties with forced gaiety;
no luncheons where everyone talks at once
and I can't hear anyone.

I don't have to
or even *I don't want to*
are reason enough for not doing.

I go where I want
but only there.

Does life go on?

Jean said
life goes on until it doesn't
and then
we shall see.

Barbara insists
there is life after death.
You'll be surprised, she says.
You'll see.

But I hold fast to my disbelief
even though
if I am right
no one will see.

LIFE AND DEATH

When my friend Gene could no longer
fight the cancer, he fought dying.
It wasn't death he feared.
It was ending his existence.

My father held life more loosely
having learned its minimal value.
He took to his bed in anticipation
and didn't have to wait long.

My mother, having lived
as much as she dared
and as long as she cared to,
welcomed her release.

As for me,
I hope my grip on life won't loosen.
I don't plan to welcome death.

In The Waiting Room

A MONTH IN THE CALENDAR
OF AN OCTOGENARIAN

Wednesday June 5 – Primary care doctor
Thursday June 6 – Audiologist
Friday June 7 – Dentist
Monday June 10 – Neurologist
Tuesday June 11 – Blood test
Wednesday June 12 – Nutritionist
Friday June 14 – Ultrasound
Monday June 17 – Podiatrist
Tuesday June 18 – Dentist
Wednesday June 19 – Hematologist
Thursday June 20 – Pulmonologist
Friday June 21 – Homeopathist
Monday June 24 – Dermatologist
Wednesday June 26 – Cardiologist
Thursday June 27 - Primary care doctor
Friday June 28– Blood test

Wednesday July 4 – Independence Day

It's not about forgetting

I forget things all the time
– names, especially –
Daniel Day Lewis,
Moon for the Misbegotten.
They aren't lost,
just temporarily misplaced.
They return when no longer needed.

It's not about forgetting;
it's about losing.
Glasses slip out of my fingers.
Playing cards stick together.
Stairs grow steeper.
I don't bend down
without holding on.

My brain slows, is easily distracted.
I forget what I mean to do
as soon as I think of something else.
I still drive
but keep the radio off.
No CDs to grab my attention.

I no longer schedule activities
two days in a row;
I need the rest in between.

It's not about forgetting.
It's about losing.

Losing
and never getting back.

ON FINDING MY WAY

I am geographically challenged.
No sense of direction,
no internal GPS
to keep me from losing my way.

It's a form of dyslexia, I explain
to those who take direction in stride.
I blame it on growing up in a city
where north-south intersects with east-west
in a precise grid.

When I was a child in the city
I wandered confidently.
Today, a senior in the suburbs,
despite Google Maps and GPS,
I roam cautiously.

FAMILY DISORDER

My grandmother wore
a cumbersome hearing aid;
a twisted wire led from her earpiece
to a battery pack clipped to her belt.
It didn't help a lot,
and she was always asking "wie?"
(the German equivalent of "what?")

My father, like Bartleby the Scrivener,
preferred not to,
thereby missing much of what was said.

My ears, too, are failing.
The hearing aids I wear reluctantly
are almost invisible.
Although the technology has vastly improved
since my grandmother's day,
I share her frustration.
"What?" is my most frequent utterance.
I hear words but can't always decipher them.
The phone, especially the cell, is a challenge.
Music – always my joy and refuge –
has become muddy.

"You'll never grow deaf,"
assures my audiologist
as she once again makes adjustments.
I try to hear her.

EXCUSE ME

Scuse me!
Hansi and I shouted,
newly arrived three-year-olds
exuberantly tasting
our first English words,
happy to bump into people
for an excuse to say
scuse me!

Excuse me?
I say now,
exuberance having long since
turned to frustration
as my hearing deteriorates.

Excuse me?

Hair today

Eighty-four years old and still
my hair is salt and pepper gray.
How long do I have to live
before my hair turns white?

Gray is so – nondescript –
a middle stage for middle age.
Where's the distinguished white
that's due someone my age?
My face – respectful –
acknowledges my years.
Why can't my hair?

I'm too old to be
prematurely white
but surely
maturely white
will still come.

Physical therapy

One foot directly in front of the other
heel to toe – wobbling –
I try to walk a straight line.
Surprisingly difficult.
My body tends to veer.
Focus, Sheela says,
but my body jeers.

Then, standing stork-like – no hands –
for an interminable sixty seconds
is a shutout:
wobble – one, balance – zero.

I do much better with machines and weights
to strengthen my weakening body parts.
I admit I'm prone
to lying down or sitting,
not standing or walking.
I supinely go for easy.

I need to focus to find a balance
between wobble and easy.
Then I won't have to focus
on my balance.

IDLE QUESTIONS

First one foot
then the other.
Yes, but which one first?

Habit, it seems,
takes over conscious thought.
When I put on a pair of pants
my right foot goes first;
when I put on my shoes
it's the left.

If I try to change the order
it feels somehow unnatural.
Who, or what,
is in charge here?

I imagine a tiny pair of pants
sitting on one side of my brain,
a miniature shoe on the other.
But which?

Does this make me
left- or right-brain dominant?
It's a muddle, but clearly
what's dominant
isn't me.

Alert

My medical alert pendant
is more alert than I am.
It hangs around my neck
day and night, even in the shower.

I can almost forget it's there
except when I accidentally hit the button
and I hear a disembodied voice:
Ruth, did you fall? Do you need help?

And each time I answer
sheepishly
I didn't mean it.
I'm fine.

I am reminded of the boy who cried wolf
who also didn't mean it,
but unlike that hapless boy
my alert will always get me help.

My doctor has become a patient

Once she was a patient doctor
but now she is a doctor patient.
Not an inpatient,
she still doctors part time.

But her illness
is full time.

She is impatient
to end her patienthood,
impatient to doctor full time again.

Her patients are sad for her
sad to see her headscarf,
sad to see her tired look,
impatient to see her healthy again,
to see her smile.

Her patients send wishes.
They have hopes
and so does she.

Unreliable memory

It is a mystery to me
how my memory
displays knowledge
I didn't know I had.

Gene Hackman, I'll answer
about a film I never saw
      or
I'll correctly identify Barber's Adagio,
a piece of music I've heard only rarely.

The answers come out of my mouth
without conscious thought –
a program that runs in background
until a random keyword
copies and pastes it on my tongue.

     And yet
ask me about a book
I just read
or what I did yesterday
and my program is in sleep mode.

MEMORY LIFE

I remember
my little red tricycle
sitting under my grandfather's piano
in the villa in Hietzing.
(We moved there after the nazis
took over the Ringstrasse apartments.)
Nonsense, said my mother.
Your tricycle was blue
and it never would have been
permitted under the piano.
Still, I see the scene.

I remember
jumping over park benches
to flee nazis in the Stadtpark.
Never happened, my mother said.
You must have been dreaming.
Still, I feel the fear.

I remember
my hand flying out in frustration
landing on my small daughter's backside.
You never hit me, Mom, she insists now.
Still, I feel the shame.

FROZEN

I try to remember how I felt
at various moments in my life
but I can only imagine it.

What did I feel when I saw
this tall toothless stranger
who claimed to be my father?

How did I feel in high school
where I was no longer the smartest
kid in the class?

What did I feel about being pregnant,
about John's concerts,
Karen's plays?

My memory is more brain than mind;
it stores events
catalogs people into time slots.

I have frozen my feelings
from my memory
the way I once froze them from my life.

SNAPSHOT COLLECTION

My childhood memories are not videos
with plot and forward motion,
each a story to tell when summoned,
but rather a collection of unrelated snapshots,
outtakes from long-ago scenes:
some underexposed
with faces hard to discern;
some little more than shadows.

Several are overexposed,
frequently examined,
smudged with greasy fingers.

IN THE WAITING ROOM

Mrs. West waits
in her wheelchair
head resting
on her right shoulder
a handkerchief
snowy as her hair
tucked into her neckline.

In well pressed khakis
left pants leg
pinned up
Mr. Klein sits
crutches slung across
the back of his chair.
His right foot taps
to his tuneless whistle.

Mrs. Robinson
swollen ankles
lapping unlaced Keds
moves ponderously
toward an empty seat.
A navy and white Yankees cap
partially covers
iron gray fuzz.

On the big TV
in the corner
Carly and Julia fight
over who is more married to Jack
as the world turns.

NIGHT SHIFT

Every two hours
like an old-time
night watchman
I go about my appointed rounds

to the bathroom.

Two o'clock and all's well.

Family
Walls

VIENNA BLOOD

Yesterday we watched
the New Year's concert from Vienna.
We watch it every year.
And every year
the concert leaves me unsettled.

The Strauss waltzes, polkas, marches
are infectious:
The Beautiful Blue Danube,
Vienna Blood,
The Radetzky March;
so familiar, so charming.
The Fledermaus overture brings smiles.

And yet
every year
I feel anger and sadness.
It's the nostalgia and heartbreak
of my parents
that has seeped into my veins.

On TV Hugh Bonneville gushes on
about the elegance of Vienna's past.
I don't recognize these rococo relics.
The beautiful blue Danube was brown
the last time I saw it,
the ancient castles along its banks crumbling.

Still, for the length of the concert
I feel the frothy heritage
of the world we lost.
My second-hand Vienna blood feels real.
So does the loss.

THE RADIO

It was the obituary of
Ruth Duskin Feldman
that brought it all back.

Ruthie Duskin – just my age –
Joel Kupperman, The Quiz Kids,
Edgar Bergen,
Fred Allen,
on the old Emerson radio.

Mom and Dad in their armchairs
and I
listening together
to the mental wizardry of
the Quiz Kids;
I wanted to be one.
Laughing together
at Charlie McCarthy's antics,
Senator Klaghorn's bluster.

Listening together,
laughing together.
For those moments
we did what families do.

Peace

In the uncertainties of the dark
I fought sleep
and its accompanying nightmares.
It was music that settled me.

Music from the radio
in the living room
where my parents
made a space for peace,
a peace that drifted down the hall
borne by Beethoven and Mozart.

It was
and is
one of their best gifts to me:
a refuge,
a consolation
for the hard times.

LUCKY

Once in a while
I read, see or hear something
that reminds me
suddenly and viscerally
how lucky I am to be alive.
How easily it could have been otherwise.

If I had not had
a great aunt in America
I could not have escaped
the nazi horror.
My life story would have been
extremely short.

But here I am
not yet at the end of a long life
and happy with it.

To my dad
WHO LEARNED TO STAND IT

When my knees ache
and I'm tempted to get off the treadmill
I think of you

When I feel finicky
about food not to my taste
I think of you

When I toss in sleeplessness
on my king-sized bed
I think of you

Whenever in my comfortable life
I'm tempted to take the easy way
I think of you

You, who had to slave beyond exhaustion
subsist on unspeakable slops
sleep on shared wooden bunks

Dachau   Buchenwald
places I can't even imagine
no matter how hard I try

You said you learned
what you can stand
You stood it

came back,
brought it with you

and taught it to me

SURVIVAL

What did it cost you, Mom,
to cast off your leper's rattle
your yellow star?

What iron determination
enabled you to function
day after day
month after month
not knowing
through an unending war
if anyone survived in
what you still called home?
Your parents, brothers, cousins.
So many,
but all just names to me.

When there is no choice, you said,
you just go on.

Yes
but what did it cost you?
What did it cost us?

RED ROVER, RED ROVER*

They didn't talk much about it,
those who got out, I mean.
Were they protecting us?
Just trying to put it behind them?
Waiting for us to ask?
It was a language we didn't have.

We always say got out
not escaped, or fled or even released.
Just got out
as though there was no human agency
        involved.
Much silence is buried in that phrase.

Come over is another, as in
when did you come over?
A substitute for
when and how did you survive?

Red rover, red rover,
just come over.

    * a children's game in which players form two
opposing lines; one team calls an individual from the
opposing team to attempt to break through their line:
Red Rover, Red Rover, we call (name) to come over.

READING WOMAN*

perches on the edge
of her tufted chair, her propped head
heavy with upswept hair.
Does she read for respite
from demands on her lady life?
Maybe her eyes are closed,
not merely cast down
at her book.

She is
perfectly posed to show
poise, repose, and yet
how constrained her Victorian life;
as confined as the girdle
girding her hips.
She is Nora, still asleep.
I want to open her door.

I was her sister, with less luxuriant hair.
Reading helped me hide, confine my life,
ignore the knocking on my door.
Admitting no one, it was
as uncomfortable a perch
as the edge of that green tufted chair.

* on viewing a reproduction of *Repose* by Jacques
     Cancaret

ON READING *THE LANYARD* BY BILLY COLLINS

Billy describes
braiding thin plastic strips into a lanyard
and I am back in summer camp
and the joy of eight weeks away from home.

I feel the slickness of that plastic
    in what was otherwise boring arts and
        crafts;
feel the excitement of color war,
    the heartbreak of being on the blue
    team when my best friend was on the
        white;
feel the relief of my bat connecting with a
        softball,
    the challenge of running uphill to first base
    on our slanting ball field.

I smell the unmistakable kitchen odors
    of milk, peanut butter, and sour dishrags;
hear the raucous voices of hungry campers
    waiting for indifferent food;
hear those voices sweetly singing *Taps*
    at Sunday night campfires.

I couldn't wait to become a counselor,
    whistle dangling importantly from the
    blue and white lanyard around my neck.

FAMILY WALLS

We were a family of three
in an apartment of walls.

He let no one in
but left his door cracked,
in case I tried to push it open.

She recognized none of our boundaries
but guarded her little bit of privacy.
When I intruded
she shut me out.

What can a child understand?
I secured my borders,
built my walls to last.

GIFT

My mother's desires were mostly unfulfilled.
My father's failures were often tallied,
treasured instruments of taunting.

But this mismatched couple could laugh,
separately and together,
> at life
> at their surroundings
> at themselves.

It was a survival technique.

It was a relief valve.

It was a gift.

EPIPHANY

The other day
I had an epiphany,
(if the word can apply
to the musing of a secular Jew)
a sudden insight
that put my dad in a different light.

What I had always seen
and condemned
as his passive personality
I now saw as inner strength.

One of his few utterances
about his Holocaust experience was
I learned what I can stand.
And *survive* was his subtext.
Nothing short of those horrors
would he allow to rouse him.

He didn't shrink passively
from my mother's taunts,
he just brushed them off
like pesky flies,
didn't let them sting.

CHILDREN IN LOVE

When we came to you
hand in hand
two 20-year olds
wanting to marry

you must have known
that our chances were dismal.
You didn't know him;
I hardly knew him.

Why were you both so accepting?
Why didn't you object,
counsel us to wait?

Were you so bewildered
by your American daughter
that you didn't or couldn't
speak up?

Was it relief
at handing me off?

Where were you
and why weren't you there?

LOVE LIGHT

I am reading this poem by flashlight;
I am supposed to be asleep.
I may not know all the words
but I hear its music.

I am reading this poem
in front of the whole sixth grade class.
I think I mispronounced something
but I keep going.

I am reading this poem in a letter
from my love who is very far away.
The poem and the letter are full of promises.

I am rereading the poem
and the letter by moonlight.
The broken promises
make my eyes sting.

About the Other Woman

Unlike Circe
she didn't let her season end.
Shameless
she trailed after him
children in tow
not satisfied until he broke
the bonds of his marriage
set her up in his second.

Not that he was an innocent
in this game of musical marriage beds.

She should have realized
that vows, once broken,
are more easily broken again.
The music stopped
and she was out
displaced
by number three.

And yet there she was again
not very much later.

No, she didn't let her season end
but I guess he liked her better
as the other woman
than as his wife.

To my long-dead ex-husband

Strange.
Now, when you come to me
in dreams
it's either as you first were,
young, loving,
hungry for a place in the world

or

as you never were to me,
a casual friend,
helpful when needed,
a bystander.

Three Little Words

HOW CAREFULLY WE NAMED YOU

How carefully we named you
John, Karen,
so un-refugee
so American
so safe.

As if your given names
could obscure the six-pointed star
in our last. (We toyed with
changing that
but your grandfather,
who owned the name
shamed us out of it.)

As if denying our history
could smooth your journeys.

As if your journeys were ours to control.

DIVORCE

... like the child lent us a while / who holds one hand of yours // and one of mine ....
Linda Pastan, *Consolations*

I grieve
not for what was
but for what wasn't there –
the hand-in-hand comfort
our children lost
before they were old enough
to remember it.

I grieve
for not having had
the reassurance
that my hand wasn't the only one
holding them up
    holding me up too.

They were children
for such a short while.
Couldn't you have waited?

Boundless

I was so lucky
with two beautiful, healthy babies.
I was awed by my boundless love for you both.
Happy that my hugs and kisses
and a "bangaid"
could cure your hurts.

Today
my love remains boundless
but my curative power has been vanquished.
My darling daughter,
if only my love were bandage enough
to cure your monstrous hurt.

THREE LITTLE WORDS

It was their era
and their upbringing.
Of all that was unsaid
in my childhood home
the biggest absence
was I love you.
It wasn't something that one said.

So, in turn, I left an absence
for my children,
assumed they knew
I loved them.
as my parents would have assumed
if they had thought about it.

And I,
thinking about it decades later,
still have to remind myself.
It isn't something that I say enough.

COMFORT ACROSS THE MILES

My dad the fixit man
could fix just about anything.
John seems to have inherited the talent.

The older I get
the less I trust myself to fix anything,
the more I need help.

John lives 3,000 miles away
but is always available to troubleshoot
by phone or internet.

When he visits he expects
a "need help here" list waiting for him;
there usually is.

His help is always within reach
even when he is not.

PENTIMENTO

I see traces of myself
in Karen,
her eyes the same startling sapphire
as in my family.

But I see more than a physical resemblance:
what was a spark in me
she fanned into
passionate flame.

I read Friedan, Steinem;
she marched.

I preached politics at the kitchen table;
she knocked on doors.

I climbed a few rungs on the ladder;
she coaches corporate leaders.

Our difference is one of generation
and intensity.

She credits me with the sparks
and I'm proud to claim them.
I admire her courage
and cheer her from the sidelines.

HINDSIGHT

I used to think
my mode was reactive, defensive,
an ad hoc approach to my daily wars;
valiant, but ultimately weak,

and yet

professionally
I acted *as if*
and I *became*.
I smashed a few
low-hanging glass ceilings

but brought the splinters home.
There, I used to think,
I just acted *as if*.

I didn't see
that I also *became*
at home.

Writing
Class

My afterlife

After the kids grew up
after I came out
after I retired

my writing became poems

MORNING TAPPING

As the days grow longer
the red-headed woodpecker
adjusts his clock
starts his tap tap tapping earlier.

Six A.M. today
and I
obedient
drag myself out
of my comfortable bed.

Once it was my mother
who woke me insistently
when I was far less obedient.
Later I turned into my mother
to rouse my children.

I like being up early.
It's the getting up that's hard.
I sit at my computer
coffee at hand
and begin my
tap tap tapping.

Process

I give myself the space
close my door
turn off the phone
prime the pump, so to speak,
by reading –
today it's Hirshfield –
find a prompt that speaks to me

but nothing speaks back.
My pump drips drivel.

I think with envy of Stafford's
poem a day.

I write about not writing.

To Linda Pastan with envy

I open Carnival Evening at random:

> *I place one word slowly*
> *in front of the other*
> *like learning to walk again*
> *after an illness.*

That even you fight

> *the white page*
> *with its hospital corners*

cheers me.

I would like to claim this image
but it is yours
along with your
flute-like gladiola,
your *poets falling like leaves,*
your images too perfect
for me to borrow.
Even your writer's block
is a poem.

You mock your
hospital-cornered page
while mine
curls up
and laughs at me.

Songs of silence

Sometimes I pretend
to be writing
and I sink
into my silence.

Somewhere in that silence
there is a whiff of lilacs.
A word falls onto my page
like a teardrop,
then another.

Somewhere in my silence
I am not pretending.

IMITATION

I am reading
Kay Ryan
and so
my normally
short lines
become
even
short-
er.

WRITING CLASS

At the still point
of my reeling brain
a perfect poem
hides.
But as the clock
ticks away
the allotted time
my cloudy mind
is flooded with
irrelevance.

If I could thread
words with my pen
like cotton
into a needle
I could sew up
this assignment
with time to spare.

Our changing language

I haven't liked you yet
I told my daughter apologetically.
She,
woman of the 21st century,
took no offense.
She knew I meant her page
not her person.

POETIC NONSENSE

My foot measures a pentameter.
I would wear rimas,
but they're too terza for my feet.

It's spring.
In spite of aphids
and anapests,
my dactyls are blooming
and iamb sneezing
and coughing.
I'll have to take a trochee
to avoid enjambment.

MY DOCTOR TAKES A WRITING CLASS

There's a whole world out there,
she says,
where they don't
          talk only about
          disorders
          infection
          stroke
          fever
          flu.

My doctor takes a writing class
and finds
                    a blossoming orchid
          a telegram from a heart in exile
the smoke and fog of a December afternoon

and
                    a red wheelbarrow.

A VISIT TO EMILY DICKINSON

I knock gently
aware of her sensibilities.
No answer.
I knock again.

A soft voice asks
who's there?
I give my name.

Are you nobody?
she asks.

Of course, I answer.
I'm totally unknown.

She opens the door.
I am nobody too, she says.

She's wearing her usual
gauzy virginal white.
She seems to float in it.
As she glides up the stairs, she says,
over her shoulder,
I can talk only briefly.
It's how I write.

Her room is as virginal
as her gown.
She sits at an old school desk
A stack of very small sheets of paper
contains all her poems.

She points me to a child's chair
and continues:
If you have a story for me
tell it slant.
I hate the obvious.
And be concise.
No longer than a tweet.

She picks up her cell phone
and texts a few lines.
See, she says,
you can tell a life
in 144 characters.
And you must have characters.

I clear my throat
cross my legs
which reach my chin
in that small chair.

Do you know the story of Alice?
I ask her.
I think we ate the wrong cookie.
Don't be smart
she snaps at me.

A three-note chime goes off.
She stands,
smoothes the skirt
of her virginal white gown
and shows me to the door.
As I leave she whispers
You really are nobody.

WAITING FOR TECH SUPPORT

Yesterday I spent my afternoon
listening to elevator music
interspersed with

Please continue to hold.
Your call will be answered
in the order it was received.

I don't know which offended me the most:
the syntax, the music, or the wait.

THE DIFFICULTY OF ENDINGS

Sometimes a phrase, a situation,
maybe an image
is all it takes
to jumpstart a poem:

> a red wheelbarrow
> a wet dog
> a hand-knitted sock

and the middle
writes itself.

But
to sum it all up
in an image
maybe a phrase

to muddle the poem

to turn its idea around
like a puppy circling its bed

there's the difficulty

and the art.

Hiatus

My book is finished
published
I've done it

life is calm
easy
I'm all caught up

not much to do
peaceful
spring has sprung

I sit on the patio
sunbathe
read The New Yorker

But

something is missing.

Where is the unease – the
nagging
need to write?

Where's the focus – the
intensity
the satisfaction in finding just the right word?

Is it the writing I miss
or
that glow from having written well?

Do I still have something to say?

Night
Light

ELEGY

The pond is still, placid –
barely a ripple to roil its surface –
surrounded by sentinels, pine and spruce,
whose mirror image echoes the stillness.

On cue this spring
green has returned to the grass
in a verdant collar around the pond,
but not to the aspens.

Thinned by angry winter winds
they mourn their losses,
stand mute, gray
against a sorrowing sky.

NIGHT LIGHT

At dusk
the shadow of the day
creeps across bare birch branches.
Twigs stick out like rude fingers.

The day's moods are stark in silhouette
but moonlight softens the landscape,
prepares the way for
a warmer light.

Backyard family

Yesterday I counted
twelve does and yearlings in our backyard.
We watch the young bucks
play-fighting.
They push back on each other's faces,
antlers having barely sprouted,
then stop to graze.

The deer have forged a trail
from the little strip of woods
across the backyard, past the house,
and across the front
into our suburban street
where they seem to have learned
to watch for cars.

Now, in February,
they wear their winter-gray coats
We worry: will they find enough forage?
Somehow they survive eating bare branches.

In spring there will be new fawns
their tan coats still spotted
Their moms keep them close
through the summer.
We see them in pairs, doe and fawn,
the fawns growing friskier.

Occasionally even a mighty stag
joins the family.
They are our year-round entertainment
and a constant joy.

PEBBLES ON THE BEACH

I walk on the beach
resolved to pick up
no more than one stone
one reminder
of the importance of this place.

But life's choices are hard enough.
Why limit myself
in the midst of this abundance
where each seems to hold its own significance.

Soon I will need to add a room
to hold all that gives me space.

SUITE IN THREE STANZAS

The robins in our yard
are very wise.
Even the late ones
catch juicy worms.
They nurture their nestlings
then let them go.

As I stand in line
at Trader Joe's
a stranger approaches,
hands me a bouquet
of tea roses and tulips.
Why? I ask.
Because you look like you deserve it.

No matter how many books I give away
my bookshelves are overloaded.
To reread all my books
would take more years than I have left
yet I keep buying more.

ODE TO MY MOCHA ICED COFFEE

I ordered it by mistake
on a hot June day
expecting black coffee
splashed with a streak of chocolate over ice.
To my chagrin, I received instead
espresso and chocolate syrup
half drowned in milk.

And I tasted it and it was good.

Not just good;
it was the madeleine of iced coffees.
It was as good – almost –
as the frappés I slurped in Greece
under another hot sun
surrounded by a babble of
emphatic syllables I couldn't decipher.

Oh my wonderful mocha iced coffee.
It made my happy day perfect
not only by its chocolatey coffee
but by bringing back
an even more blissful taste and time.

I look with gratitude
at my empty plastic cup
straw sticking into the air
with only a few brown stains
to remember what it held so gloriously.

Its gift to me
the remembrance of things past.
It brought me through this to that.

Mozart's Piano Concerto #21

I have listened to the concerto so often
the music is imprinted on my brain.
It accompanies my quiet moments
in a silvery cascade
and although my replaying is imperfect
I hear Uchida.

COMFORT

If we had a fire,
Barbara asks,
what would you try to save?
She has already planned for this.

I ponder.
Family records, photos?
What little jewelry I value?
Just you and me, I answer.
There wouldn't be time for more.

But afterwards
what would I miss?

As I simplify my life
things, just things,
are less and less important.

But oh, my books.

Even as I start to forget their contents
I wrap myself in their presence.

Down to earth

Pluto
our farthest space neighbor,
recently demoted to dwarf,
has been brought closer to earth.
Its heart-shaped mysteries
have now been seen
but it will take much study
to understand them.

Not all mysteries of the heart
can be solved by study.
Sometimes it's enough
to observe a mystery,
to know that not all is knowable.
What matters is
to keep shortening
the distance that remains.

Whoever can cry

A reflecting pool
an honoring of footprint
a defiant new tower.
Whoever can cry should come here.

Buildings have become symbols.
Names are read.
Fountains splash patriotic pieties.
Visitors cry in community,
their duty, or curiosity, satisfied,

but I am no respecter of ritual.
When ritual stands in for responsibility
I find I have no tears.

Until evening

Love, how the hours accumulate.
It seems only yesterday we bought this house,
blended households and histories
but held ourselves distinct, individual.

How wise we were
bonding without merging
each walking our own path

until evening
when we braid our hours together.

RUTH STEINBERG

   is the author of *A Certain Frame of Reference*, a collection of poems about her experiences as a child refugee from Hitler's Vienna and the implications and consequences of her history. *A Step in Time* broadened her outlook to considerations of aging, politics, travel and observations of New Yorkers in a Manhattan delicatessen.

In *Shadows, Echoes, Memories* she looks back at the history of her family in pre-World War II Vienna, at her loves, her fears, her reflections, in subjects ranging from personal history to aging to politics and travel.

She also published *Word Play,* a chapbook of her humorous verse. She is a co-author of *Counting the Stones*, and co-author and editor of *The Poets' Roundtable.*

She is a former editor of two semi-technical magazines, and before her retirement was the Director of Technical Publication at a telecommunications R&D company. She is member of the International Women's Writing Guild.

Made in United States
Troutdale, OR
02/24/2024

17943387R00070